PENGUIN BOOKS

The *Symmetry of Fish*

SU CHO is a poet and essayist born in South Korea and raised in Indiana. She has an MFA in poetry from Indiana University and a PhD from University of Wisconsin–Milwaukee. She has served as the editor in chief of *Indiana Review* and *Cream City Review*, and has served as guest editor for *Poetry* magazine. Her work has been featured in *Poetry*, *New England Review*, *Gulf Coast*, and *Orion Magazine*; the 2021 *Best American Poetry* and *Best New Poets* anthologies; and elsewhere. A finalist for the 2020 Ruth Lilly and Dorothy Sargent Rosenberg Poetry Fellowship, a recipient of a National Society of Arts and Letters award, and a two-time Pushcart Prize nominee, she is currently an assistant professor at Clemson University.

The National Poetry Series was established in 1978 to ensure the publication of five collections of poetry annually through five participating publishers. The Series is funded annually by Amazon Literary Partnership, William Geoffrey Beattie, the Gettinger Family Foundation, Bruce Gibney, HarperCollins Publishers, The Stephen and Tabitha King Foundation, Padma Lakshmi, Lannan Foundation, Newman's Own Foundation, Anna and Olafur Olafsson, Penguin Random House, the Poetry Foundation, Amy Tan and Louis DeMattei, Amor Towles, Elise and Steven Trulaske, and the National Poetry Series Board of Directors.

THE NATIONAL POETRY SERIES
WINNERS OF 2021 OPEN COMPETITION

The Symmetry of Fish by Su Cho
Chosen by Paige Lewis for Penguin Books

Harbinger by Shelley Puhak
Chosen by Nicole Sealey for Ecco

Extinction Theory by Kien Lam
Chosen by Kyle Dargan for University of Georgia Press

Ask the Brindled by Noʻu Revilla
Chosen by Rick Barot for Milkweed Editions

Relinquenda by Alexandra Lytton Regalado
Chosen by Reginald Betts for Beacon Press

The Symmetry of Fish

SU CHO
조수린

PENGUIN BOOKS

PENGUIN BOOKS
An imprint of Penguin Random House LLC
penguinrandomhouse.com

LIBRARY OF CONGRESS CATALOGING-IN-PUBLICATION DATA
Names: Cho, Su, author.
Title: The symmetry of fish / Su Cho.
Other titles: Symmetry of fish (Compilation)
Description: New York : Penguin Books, [2022]
Identifiers: LCCN 2022008438 (print) | LCCN 2022008439 (ebook) |
ISBN 9780143137252 (trade paperback) | ISBN 9780593511206 (ebook)
Subjects: LCSH: Immigrants—United States—Poetry. |
Koreans—United States—Poetry. | Families—Poetry. | LCGFT: Poetry.
Classification: LCC PS3603.H625 S96 2022 (print) | LCC PS3603.H625 (ebook) |
DDC 811/.6—dc23/eng/20220517
LC record available at https://lccn.loc.gov/2022008438
LC ebook record available at https://lccn.loc.gov/2022008439

Printed in the United States of America
2nd Printing

Set in Adobe Garamond Pro
Designed by Catherine Leonardo

for my parents
김민숙 & 조규호
Min & Andrew

for my siblings
조수빈 & 조의현
Michelle & David

and for my grandparents
조익환 & 송순조
김광수 & 강연님

CONTENTS

II.

III.

HOW TO SAY WATER

Pucker your lips like a fish, your tongue
a cautious eel, pushing its head
to the roof of your mouth.

Breathe through your nose as you practice
the silence of this exercise.
Don't bite yourself

trying to make water with sounds of agreement
from your chest. Yes, that *mm*—
simultaneously creates

a small gap between those tense lips.
Tilt your head back, a finger
on your throat.

Please, start from the top and try to follow
along. I wish you could borrow
my body to say water.

This is the easiest way I can help you say 물
because I could never help my parents
say *girl, ice cream, parfait.*

I.

가시: (N) THORN, SPLINTER, FISH BONE

Home for a panfried mackerel dinner,

    my mother watches my chopsticks stumble

around the 가시. I am full after a few bites.

    I remember a story. When I was a baby

I choked on 가시 at my grandparents' house. My dad

    wasn't there. They yelled at her

for not inspecting each flaky bit of fish I put

    in my clumsy mouth, not teaching me

the maneuvering of spiky slivers with my tongue,

    how to place the needles next to my plate,

extract white meat clean. Since then, she peels & holds

    skeletons above our meal—fossils before me.

Still, I am bad at peeling bone from fish,

    skin from pears. If you can't peel the skin

of a pear in a thin spiral with a fruit knife

you can't get married. You can have

nothing if you can't offer a man fruit.

My mouth dripping with SunGold kiwi,

I tell my love these stories, laughing—

here we are! Me spooning the yellow center

into my mouth, cupping the furry layer

in my palm; him standing over the sink

sinking his teeth into the skin. What would

my mother say? Once, a splinter burrowed into the meat

of my thumb, and I kept it there for weeks.

Told my parents the splinter came out on its own

while I hoped my body would absorb the slender spear

and disappear the 가시 painlessly.

THE OLD MAN IN WHITE HAS GIVEN MY MOTHER A RIPE PERSIMMON AGAIN

But this time she is not pregnant. In this dream, the fruit's puckered
skin droops with sweetness in his palm, beckoning her to witness
this precious gift. She insists that this was for me but that remains
impossible. My body is special, she whispers over the phone. I must
cherish this landscape because all the persimmons tumbling down
the hills and gathering into the valley belong to me. The orange fruits
with verdant leaves are hard and glistening because they are not
meant to drop so soon, though others dangle heavy on their branches.

But my island is full of maiden ghosts who hover close to fallen fruit.
When the longing to press them between their thighs is too great, together,
they dive into the ocean and hunt for clams, cull seaweed to dress themselves,
holding breaths before breaking surface with their bounty. My grandmother's voice
is in every kitchen, asking me to pluck a husband from the ground if I see one worthy
as she surveys the box of collapsed acorn persimmons with a spoon in hand.

But I am always surrounded by oceans, the crunch of unripened bodies between
my teeth with the ghosts patrolling my shores, making way for this maiden voyage.

TONIGHT I DISCOVER ARCHIPELAGOES

In the dip between my hip and pelvis
a patch of skin void of my rosy beige.
I press a finger against the supple

surface—the way my mother pressed
kisses on the black dot on the heel
of my left foot, assuring me that

she would find me by lifting
the foot of every child—
pretending to have never seen my face.

Against my finger, I hear a metronome
pulse I still can't keep in time with. Some nights
I want a hand above my left breast, thrumming

a beat to keep me warm. I turn to examine
the mirror for more pockets of discovery
only to find a stretch of colorless islands wrecked

from my lower back to my shoulders as if
I went to erase my black dot but forgot where it was.

HELLO, MY PARENTS DON'T SPEAK ENGLISH WELL, HOW CAN I HELP YOU?

Are you the head of the household?
Because I am
Calling about the census—
Dear, I need to speak with an adult
Even if they don't speak English well.

For every call like this, my mother
Gestures wildly as if we
Haven't done this a million times.
I'm sorry, I say back to the voice.
Just do it, just once, and I shrug, listen to my mom saying she's sorry,
Korean, yes. She stumbles over the practiced phrase, Please
Listen to my daughter,
My English
No good.

Once I called her stupid for
Packing my field trip lunch with
Quick sesame rice balls even though that's what I
Requested. That isn't true. I called her
Stupid after she hit me for low grades in English class.

The truth is, I hated my friends
Upset over the sesame smell sprawled over the
Verdant lawns of the IMAX theater. A field trip, perfect
Weather. The expensive sticky rice, stones in my stomach.
X-rays of what I eat at home scattered for the school to see.
Yet twenty years later, I am on the phone in a different time
Zone, speaking for my mother, how we just want some accountability.

SHE AROSE

From a bed of woodchips
behind a plastic rock climbing wall.

From Easter tulle and chiffon
and ribbons at the waist to school

every day until she shed that skin
and lived in jean skorts, in fog

because she couldn't believe
that something visible would be

impossible to reach. She lived
in an army of garden snails

for their soft suction and sleepover
pranks. Shook off those creatures

to find she bloomed of grass stains,
soccer shin bruises, basketball elbows.

When those trophies faded,
she discovered her softness,

the constant blush of skin, until she forgot
what color she was to begin with—

until she made click-clacks
of the bicycle beads' neon spectrum.

Her eyes never left the front wheel—
in love with how it blurred into an unnameable hue.

DIORAMA THIS

collection of Forever American flag stamps
      inside a blue plastic book with crinkled vellum

mini Thanksgiving float for the Cumberland
      Elementary School parade made of unbaked
      polymer clay thudding apart with the first tug

birthday party at Great Skates
      the center rink when the DJ says chow
      instead of Cho

sticky rice paste instead of Elmer's glue
      to fasten paper chains of once-a-year metallic origami
      to celebrate the New Millennium with

Honorable Mention for Indiana's second-grade
      poetry contest about a girl
      who will invent a waterless shower
      and a blue plastic pill that can cure anything

WINTERS IN QUEENS

We sleep on the heated floors of the church's
        nursery room every winter because

something is wrong with my mother's
        green card application. We stack

Spice Girls gum and tearjerker gumballs
        each day to prepare for the trip back

to Indiana. The dogs chained outside the gates
        yip as my brother and I gaze

past the sanctuary's one-way mirror. In the ocean
        of red carpet and crosses, a lone woman

prays so hard that I swear I can hear her through
        this soundproof glass. She sways forward

and back like a thick spring uncoiled. More women
        enter and when perms are loosened,

dabbing at their eyes, I realize that the woman
        is my mother. She can't see me but I duck

into the sleeping bag. In the car ride back home,
        our bodies still buzz. We munch on vanilla

crème cookies from the gas station and make crosses
     with the Slim Jims in our laps. When we hit

empty cornfields, we hit our heads against the seat
     imagining ourselves chanting *Ju-Yuh, Father, Our Father.*

ABECEDARIAN FOR ESL IN WEST LAFAYETTE, INDIANA

A is for apples shipped fresh off the
Boat. At two p.m. we left math to go where
Children are taught
Differences between
English and English at home.
For example, Sun-Ah, who named herself Sunny,
Grabbed blue pills from a plastic bag,
Held the medicine in her palm. Teachers called me in—
Ibuprofen, I say. I am seven,
Just learned the word because Sunny sputtered
Korean that they're painkillers.
Look, English was my second language but
My tongue was new.
Never had to teach me to curl my *r*'s
Or how to say *girl*, *blueberries*, *raspberries*. In second grade, I
Played Peter Rabbit's mother rabbit, still don't
Quite know how that happened or even
Remember what my lines were.
Still, when the Chicago Field Museum unveiled Sue
The T. rex, I was Sue the dinosaur; before that, Sue who lived in an old shoe.
Usually I said, "Yes, like the T. rex without the useless *e* at the end."
Versions of my selves in ESL exist but I was held there after proficiency.
Who else would translate for the teachers, my parents, and Sunny's parents?
X was for xylophones, X-rays, and now xenophobia.
Yes, that's too on the nose, but things on your nose are hardest to see.
Z is for a zero, zigzagging between classrooms to say she has a fever, she misses home.

밤: (v) TO GIVE DEATH; (n) CHESTNUT, NIGHT

I clung to my grandfather's back
like a beetle on a sesame leaf
every time he leapt over chasms
to take me mountain raspberry hunting.

He hit trees with a long wooden rod
and chestnuts fell from the sky.
His palms broke the spindly shields
when knives couldn't split the burr.

Once, we picked out the prettiest chicken
and the strangled squawks bubbled
into the best chicken porridge I've ever had.
A trellis of buzzing flypaper always smacked

his forehead and he never flinched. Tombstones
line the terraced hills next to fields of soybeans
and tobacco. Is there no magic from my mouth
when I say that my grandfather is dead—

that I still don't really care? My mouth
dressed in fried bread crumbs, like the fish
on the table—a low *ah* escaping my lips
curling over my teeth to say 밤.

AFTER THE BURIAL, THE DEAD TAKE EVERYTHING THAT BURNS

My grandmother picks up
the bottom of her white hemp
mourning dress and hurls
a fluorescent green bottle of soju
into the fire. The great bier
with magenta and neon yellow
streamers cracks inside the smoke.
Facing the marble headstone
are pastel rice cakes
and apples stacked five high.
Pouring soju into ceramic glasses,
she toasts to the harvest,
tosses wedding portraits,
fine linens, cabbages, and his
work pants into the pyre,
and sits in front of the marble table
with a bowl of rice and drink, waiting
for him to pick up his chopsticks and eat.

GRATITUDE FOR HIS HANDS

that snapped chicken necks
    cracked garlic cloves
    shooed away wild dogs
    yanked weed after weed
    pierced this earth with a shovel
rest at his sides—underneath his harvest.

ACCORDING TO MY FATHER, PEACHES WARD OFF SPIRITS

On the marble
slab are geometric
offerings of apples,
plums, and pears.
My parents bow
toward the tumulus
of my grandfather
and bump into the plums,
not noticing them
falling off the table.
I gather them
in my shirt
but don't want to get
too close.
The plums are days
old, mushy and warm.
A fly buzzes
in my ear,
making me drop
them—one
by one they roll
toward the tumulus
and burrow into the ground.

WE ARE ALL DYING, SLOWLY

My grandmother drapes a blanket
around a mahogany picture frame
of my grandfather, who died decades ago,
but she is so happy he's home. So happy
that she pinches my aunts' arms
for not greeting him properly.
As if he has stepped out
of the frame and as if he is simply
sleeping on the couch, farting up a storm,
making all of us skitter away pinching
our noses. My grandmother is back
on her homemade yogurt kick because
he likes it. Later, there is a baby-blue
bedtime hat to keep his head warm
to make sure they live a long life together.
But when he stops talking, she wonders
why he's mad, but it's okay because they
are in love again, and even when my aunts remove
all the framed pictures in the house,
my grandmother calls my mother to exclaim
that Su visited! How surprising! So happy
because I, too, haven't been back in a decade, too busy living
in the USA! I am on the phone, pacing away
from my parents. I say I'm glad she was happy, and when I say bye
in English, she laughs, *thank you, thank you very much,*
and my grandmother knows I wasn't really there.
But later, the big family portrait, from when I was ten,
my dad and uncle photoshopped in, my grandparents
sitting on regal chairs in the center, the many, many cousins
I don't talk to anymore surrounding them, that portrait

has been taken away from my grandmother's apartment.
I say to my mother, we were all so little, so beautiful,
and maybe they should put the picture back on her mantel
because she will have so much company, be busy for a long time,
busy making yogurt, calling every one of us to say
how delightful her day was when we visited, laughing, *thank you, thank you.*

II.

THROUGH THE FISSURES

The goats are on their sides,
skinned and draped across

a wooden table with uneven
legs. The butcheress slices

through bone with a blade
that never glints red.

Their heads are lined up,
white fur and eyes sharp.

I look at the meat on
display and think—how

tender. I know the smallest bones
hide themselves

in the plush cuts of meat.
There is a collection

of accidents jagged along the
lining of my throat, cluttered

with pin bones and pebbles.
These splinters buried under

such pleasure clatter and knock
through my teeth, desperate to get out.

A LITTLE CHEONYEO GWISHIN APPEARS IN MY KITCHEN

She snaps the heads
off dried anchovies,
their eyes a black
anthill burying my toes.

I'm breaking doenjang
with the flat head
of a metal spoon,
stirring the boomerang
silver bodies she drops.

Whenever she feels
like showing up, we cook
together. She opens
the tofu, smashes
the watery curd with her
foot, and soaks

a package of dried kelp
in the trash. The brittle
pieces like unspooling
magnetic tape.

Today, she sticks her white face
through this seaweed curtain,
red lips smeared,
whispering, *Look*

look, this is just like my hair.
Why don't you ever
brush it? She disappears.

Now she chatters about
how much salt I'll ingest
by putting that much
doenjang in, scooping
the anchovy eyes and
dumping them in the stew.

Aren't you supposed
to be bothering men?
Why don't you go
back to paradise?

She rises up. Her arms
hang like wet ropes,
head tilting until
her chin points
to the ceiling.

She cries, *Why am I
here? None of my mothers
will tell me why I am here.*

PURLICUES

for Anthony

        I pinch the space between my love's thumb and forefinger,
knowing he will jerk his hand away in pain. This is his fourth time
indigested, and this is my fourth time hopeful. Again I speak
of miraculous healings—my blood oozing black, swelling
into dark spheres, then red again.

                I pinch him again and promise to hold
the needle above a flame instead of scratching the bent tip against my scalp
like my mother. I tell him stories of the retractable needle
in a glossy mahogany tube whenever I have indigestion.

        I offer my rare supply of Korean pills that smell through
my gallon Ziploc, which turn out to just be charcoal pills.
I offer more nameless antibiotics, digestives, and cure-alls.
I offer this and perhaps the tiny pinch after.
My hope ascends

            into faith while my love remains grounded
in his body. His computer tells him that my technique seems to be rooted
in acupuncture. So I always bite his shoulder, his fingers, since I know
he will never let me prick his thumb to prove I am right.

              But I am nervous that if he finally succumbs,
offers his thumb, his blood will remain red. By the end of this poem, I am always
surprised when he says, I let you do it once before. This time, I will ask if he remembers
that *purlicue* means the end of discourse, the place between your thumb
and forefinger—where I hold you to see if you are finally ready.

TANGERINE TREES AND LITTLE BAGS OF SUGAR

My mother speaks of how she was born on an island, where a father grew a family of seven from one tangerine tree purchased from a local trader. How he saved for a plot of land & the tangerines were good—so good. My mother speaks of how a mother would travel back to Seoul alone to buy sugar—heaps of sugar in clumpy bags—bring it back to package them with ribbons and rippling clear cellophane to the people on the island who didn't know it was possible to cross the ocean. How these tangerine trees and bags of sugar birthed a brick-lined mansion, chauffeurs, and gift boxes of echoing Korean pears to each of her and her sibling's classrooms. A whole heavy box for every teacher. As I frown and complain that these pears even from Jersey aren't sweet, she tells me to be thankful and reminds me that if I can't shave the skin off these pears I will never get married. Be grateful that I get to pick this fruit. Grateful that we received a shipping box full of bruised tangerines that grew on the island when they were still alive to remind us of work. How I used to scrunch my nose at the furry bruised skin and marvel at how the peel revealed plump fruit, tasting like all the sugar and sweat carried across oceans until everyone was satisfied.

BOWL OF FAT

She rattles the oxtails in the milky
yellow soup with a wooden spoon.

The humid garage fills with a smothering
of garlic, pepper, and gasoline.

The portable gas burner wobbles every time
she stirs. With steady hands,

she skims off the yellow fat from
the surface and dumps it into a bone-

white rice bowl. She calls for me
once she is finished. Before carrying

this brimming offering inside, I ask
why she bothers to skim the fat when it takes so long.

She says it's healthier this way and asks
if I want this yellow gunk inside my body.

Before I can answer, she snaps
for me to shut the door to not

waste the cold air inside, to go
straight to the bathroom and wash my feet

because the floors are clean—
she is barefoot.

URGENT CARE

My brother scream-stumbles on the wooden deck,
banging the sliding glass door open with the other

children chanting *bee bee bee*. My mother peels
his hand from his neck, finding five welts already

hard against her finger. She lugs out the tub of
doenjang from the fridge, the salty odor

slapping the air with its weight. Her fingers
pierce the paste, slathering it thick, and

press a wet paper towel against the burnt
and swollen neck—catching light-brown water

in the creases. When they return from the hospital,
she huffs at how the doctors declared foreign substance

and possible infection. Nothing scientifically sound as
she insists how something buried and fermenting

for years can be a potent magic toward any malady.

THE SUN AND MOON BEGAN WITH A MOTHER WORKING

A torso tumbles down a hill and a tiger waits with unhinged jaws, still hungry after eating the woman's rice cakes, arms, and legs. The rice cake saved after working at the rich man's house, how she offered her arms, then only her left leg to the tiger so she could hop back to her children on the remaining right. After eating the mother, the tiger saunters to her children, still hungry. Brother and sister pray to the gods for a rope to carry them off the tree they scurried up, the sesame oil they pour down a useless deterrent. The tiger chops down the tree with an axe. The sky drops an iron chain and the siblings climb, laughing at the tiger. But even heaven can be no respite, so the sister becomes the sun and brother the moon. Not because a girl shines bright but to preserve her modesty, the rays blinding anyone who stares at her a little too long—

FERMENTED

Pepper paste stamps her
crimson. It seeps up her wrists,

forearms, elbows, so I leave.
From my room I imagine

her knee-deep in the kimchi,
nestled against

the steel bowl
of cabbages painted red.

She sprinkles the pepper flakes
like freckles speckling her skin.

She massages her temples with paste-caked hands,
kneading color into each hair

drained of its blackness.
I walk downstairs & peer into the kitchen.

Her hands—only
her hands disappear

between the flakes and minced prawns.
Pruned fingers lift each layer of leaves

lathing the kimchi
as if stroking my hair.

I twist five glass jars open,
line them up along the table,

& watch how she cradles each cabbage,
laying them down to rest in glass every winter.

쌀 OR 살: RICE OR FLESH

Here is another story
featuring rice cakes
but without their sweetness.
A mother cuts yards
of chewy, soft cylinder
rice cakes, each cut forming
even cushions.
Her son's handwriting
is abysmal, so she challenges
him to practice brushstrokes
while she slices cakes clean
in the dark.
She blows out the candles.
By dawn his words a Rorschach
spillage on paper she broke
her back to purchase. Imagine
this ends with a simple
beating, a lesson.
Don't forget about the tiger
always lurking in the woods.
The lesson is to be quiet
and obedient because good
daughters and sons are graced
with rice cakes even
while they sleep.

MY BED SHAKES AND I ASSUME THE GHOSTS ARE FINALLY GETTING ME

for Kia

But it's just an earthquake in Indiana. I like to tell
this story because it reminds me of you. We first

met in high school summer gym class, where
we turned jeans into floatation devices and tallied

bowling scores by hand. We got close in AP English
when we admitted that we read *Jane Eyre* in one evening,

how we loved the teacher's tape recording of *Macbeth*
because we really didn't understand what was supposed

to be funny. Back then, we wanted to be rappers or doctors,
and now benevolent EDM DJs in Vegas. We love to chug

coffee past eleven p.m. so we can shit a final time before
a night of dancing and waddling through snow in high heels

we bought after we broke up with our boyfriends.
The older we get, we are always late. Like to the Odesza concert

you won radio tickets to, how we shivered underneath
big blankets covered in dog hair, the outfits we picked out

months ago never seen in blurry pictures. I am writing all this
to get to what I really want to say—you are the most faithful

person I know. You believe in prayer because you believe
in ghosts, in vengeful spirits because you've seen them. Once,

you asked me if I thought you were silly for being so superstitious
and I said no—I pray when I am scared, the only time I take

in Jesus's name I pray seriously. Me trusting my mouth and you,
for good measure, hanging a picture of Jesus above the bed,

a crucifix, and even a bible on your nightstand even though
we both don't read it anymore. Here, I try to conjure images

or metaphors of our selves but I can only
remember the things we say to each other—*isn't it funny*

how every Asian girl we know is engaged or about to be engaged
to a white boy or *now we know not to trust white moms from Carmel*

because they voted for Trump or *we'd rather them smile at us while keeping*
their hate to themselves or *isn't it funny we don't go out anymore* or *this is better*

than the drunk white boys who follow us to the car all the time or *after midnight*
or *our mothers this our mothers that* or—

ODE TO PUTTING IN THE WINDOW AC UNIT

Milwaukee, Wisconsin, October 2021

We open the screenless window and bat our arms
to clear the buffet of lake gnats, flies, and knots
of insect carcasses beaded on the spiderweb
that has been growing for over a year.

There is a small, grayed husk in the right corner
of the window, and we think just maybe
that is the beginning of a wasp's nest, and with
consideration, we bat that off the window too.

We can't find the duct tape to seal off the cracks
and because there were no presents to wrap this year
I get the best Scotch tape, and there it is! The wasp
hovering where we destroyed its starter home.

The bird that started a nest in the other window returns,
the lake spiders lining the fake French doors drop down,
remind us to never open them for a breeze because they love
to wave their thick pincers hello! I am hungry, but we must

finish screwing the AC unit in place, just the one screw
because the rest are lost, and hope that the wind won't knock it off.
Our arms are shaking, weak from being inside, moving
the fridge out, lugging last year's storage from behind

our favorite appliance, hoisting the giant box of cool air
above our heads to squeeze out the kitchen, and there is dirt
everywhere, but at least we love each other
enough to know the roar of the air conditioner
lets us hold each other again.

AT AN APPLE ORCHARD IN DOOR COUNTY, WISCONSIN

In a barn, which is really a store, I stand in front of a pyramid of horseradish spreads
and everyone stares at me. The garlic mustard kraut horseradish isn't even made
here but made on Blackberry Farm in Georgia. I read each flavor profile.
Put everything I touch into my basket. From a bushel of pears, I pick one
of each color. I wait for you to come back from the bathroom and think
of the weekend I spent whispering *I haven't seen anyone like me*—wait, there!
I see a family I once knew in Purdue Village but that would be impossible
because that was over fifteen years ago. I saw their black hair, square silver
glasses, daughters in pigtails, squeaky light-up shoes. Instead of smiling,
nodding *yes, I see you*, I stare at their empty red-trim basket.
Yes, my love is white & yes, I do wonder how long our children's
eyelashes will be, what shade of brown their hair will turn in the sun.
This no longer gives me joy but a wish to watch them race each other
through the hay maze, laughing loudly at the caricature pumpkins with giant eyes.

AUBADE WITH METAL SPOON

for Michelle

We check each other's eyes
to see what kind of day
we are given. But we love
the symmetry between our faces.
Both our left eyes like our mother
and our right eyes a plush double eyelid.

To be safe, she holds the cold spoon
against her eye, the edge we use
to cut into steaming kimchi dumplings, against her lid.
She counts to thirty, asking
if anything changed, if this is worth it.

THE CHEONYEO GWISHIN MARRIES ME

My mother calls to ask if I still
sleep with my hair undone

and to tell me about the spider
she accidentally sprayed Windex on

and how she watched its legs shrivel
into its body. How it disappeared.

She likes to remind me that a ghost
in her white sobok will lie at my side,

stroke my wet tangles, and braid
my tresses into a heavy black rope.

I want to tell her there's no such thing
as ghosts but she isn't speaking

of ghosts. In bed, I touch the little cuts
on the backs of my arms from the shower

and feel a tickle of hair. My lips still
as her mane blankets my shoulders.

She coils my hair into a high bun.
The swish of the goreum from her dress

lulls me to sleep as she uses her ribbon
to pull stray hairs from my eyes.

MUG CLUB

for Maggie, Scott, and Anthony

On Tuesday nights
we meet at Brothers
for pulled porks, AMFs,
and discounted wings—
all salt, no punch.

We discuss
how our exes
are vectors, how we are
their origin points.

We insert ourselves
into a boring formula
to calculate how far
these exes will land
away from us.
The time it takes them
to spiral back after
stalling at their peak.

After another round,
we joke how we exist
inside this self-made
centrifugal force—
what tethers us
to the fear of losing
momentum, that this spinning
constant will halt.

ERGONOMICS

for Maggie

If I told you   I thought *carpal tunnel*   was *carpool tunnel*   you would
laugh   but who wouldn't   want to be stuck   inside a '97 Town and Country
      hurtling through a tunnel   detachable seats gone   sitting cross-legged   in
a circle linking arms   swaying with the curves   of the road   after an
hour   you realize   no one is driving   that there are some things
      we still don't understand   how some parts   of the lake   are easier
to paddle through   how a turtle   at the bottom   of shallow water
      looks so far away   why it's worse   to grocery shop sad than
hungry how lifting a leather couch   up a flight   of wooden stairs
      feels easy as   a pack of Spirits   on the cramped unpainted porch
      overlooking   the same strangers   walking and biking
how some don't understand   that we can miss people   next to us
how space disappears by sitting   with someone in a car   not saying
anything   because
when we step   too close to bliss   our bodies stop   to wonder   if they
have to   jump-start   our atoms again

OPEN DISKECTOMY

Carry him
on your shoulders
set him facedown
so he is numb and
sterilized by the snow
no anesthesia or metal
trays of scalpel and clamps
just your hands
and a zipper
to fasten on the back
of his neck
with your nails
cut a place
to line the zip
down the center
of his shoulder blades
grip one in place
before ripping
the metal down
skin will snag
between the teeth
but keep going
until you hit the tailbone
elbows out pull
his back apart
until you see traces
of this bone
gently stomp
on the neck
until you hear

a dull crack
with both hands
lift the spine like
bones of mackerel
drag it out
it is heavier
than you imagined
ice your hands
in the snow
fill the cavity
up with snow
fill it with bags
of rose potpourri
from your back pocket
finally undress
yourself and lie
inside this wound
crossing your ankles
twisting on your side
zipping yourself
inside the body
the only way
you know how
to fix him

THE SYMMETRY OF FISH

The head of the fish thuds
into the kitchen sink

with a splash of lettuced water.
She says, *Not this. Don't*

*marry the head or anyone
too cunning.* She saws the knife

through the tail. The muscle
springs. *Not a man*

who doesn't have a brain.
There's no meat there.

As I walk through fish markets
lined with skinned goats,

their heads on the tables,
the finned bellies glisten under

the dusty sun, jutting
proudly blue and silver.

My mother's voice asks me
if I understand, if I'll resist

the smooth talk from the fish's
mouth, his fanned tail swaying,

gifting a breeze on the back
of my neck. I prod the slick,

elastic skin, pierce him with two
fingers, and eat around the bones.

III.

REMEMBER THIS WHEN YOU'RE HUNGRY

for my grandma, whose Korean name I still can't remember

Even a ghost that eats and dies again will have better color.

How hungry we must have been to die in the ocean just to pull at its weeds, dry them, soak the leaves in sesame oil.

Bleed our hands for not even a tongueful of meat from an ungiving shell.

A bird that cries at night cries because it mourns a lover.

A bird that cries in the morning cries because it is hungry.

How do you eat like a king?

Hang the remains of last week's fish so it sways above the table.

Have a bite of rice. Chew ten times. Look at the fish. Chew ten times. Repeat.

Give thanks for anything you can put in your mouth.

WAITING IN LINE AT THE OUTLET MALL

My grandma is eighty and teaches us
how to tell the difference between
a real pearl and a knockoff.
She clacks the pearls between her teeth,
grinds down on them. She asks
if it's smooth or a little chewy.
My sister takes a handful, ready
to chomp, and Grandma slaps
her hand, tells her to not actually bite.
We're latched on to her necklace
like suckerfish at her throat.

사랑니: (N) WISDOM TEETH

The dentist says I only have
two wisdom teeth,

which are sleeping sideways
and will probably never move.

I tell my parents this and point
to the back of my mouth.

After thinking all my molars
were dead, they smile—exclaiming

that it's time to get my 사랑니
out. I point again to my wisdom teeth

because 사랑 means love,
not wisdom, in case they take

the wrong ones out.
It takes a whole car ride back

to settle on the fact that wisdom teeth
are love teeth. I ask why—

they shrug and say that's how it is.
Like the time Stacy had a sleepover,

we all talked about the garden snails
in her fish tank and later whispered

how we'd put them in Stacy's pillow.
After our mothers came to get us

past midnight, we tried to explain why
we hadn't realized that 지혜

had feelings and wondered
if anyone else found it funny

that our moms were asking us
to consider wisdom's feelings.

A CHEONYEO GWISHIN TELLS ME A STORY

A dokkaebi with a magic club in the woods comes across an old woman and man tending their garden overgrown with sesame leaves, pumpkins, and cherry tomatoes. There's a pear-shaped growth off the old man's chin. The pouch sags with each step. One night, the dokkaebi wonders if this man is hiding gold in this flesh pouch—how clever it is to hide treasures inside your body forever. Say the dokkaebi approaches and the man is laughing so hard he can't even call to his wife to see what wonder they will finally witness living here all alone. The creature demands the gold, pointing to the sack of skin, but he seems inexperienced, so the old man invites him to touch. The dokkaebi swings his club toward the man's face, and with only a cold breeze, the lump is gone and hangs from the dokkaebi's hip. The old woman emerges from the house and demands he repay them in equal measure. She points to the chestnuts on the ground and challenges him to turn them into ginseng and emeralds. With a theatrical twirl, he lifts the club and thwacks each chestnut in the dark and runs. See the old man and woman laugh together, him nuzzling his lump-free chin against hers, walking back to their bed. Say they didn't even bother looking back on the green glittering in the moonlight, ginseng roots sprawling across the clearing.

PEACH BLOSSOMS

Twenty-two yellow teeth pour out of my father's hands
and into my open hands, like an offering.

They singe my palm before singing against the xylophone
panels of the deck. The teeth sprout into peaches—

growing & rolling, the fuzzy skin grazing my calves.
My throat itches and swells, but I want to say something.

The deck croaks under this bounty. I rub my throat
and the spruce saplings chant *peaches peaches.*

The repairmen stand in the cavity, removing the last
wooden boards. A hive must have broken as they pick

bees off the ground. Bending the saplings, we search
for what made the peaches stop growing.

ODE TO THE NEW YORK HEAT WAVE

My family discovered each other in a house
during a heat wave. The five of us,

on the bare floor, trying not to touch
each other, breathe too loud, and

inching closer to the window. My sister
is the youngest and won't stop crying.

She asks if we're poor now, if she has to go
get a job. We laugh, congratulate her

for being able to see the bigger picture.
At night, my dad orders buffalo chicken pies,

vodka pies, a classic pepperoni, and as many
cold liters of Coke we want, keeping our mouths

full and quiet. We broker
bathroom time like strangers

meeting for the first time
every morning.

봉숭아: (N) GARDEN BALSAMS, TOUCH-ME-NOTS

The last time I came back from Korea was with fingernails
stained orange, scarlet, my lunulae still visible and sinking

behind my cuticles. I hoped no one would notice at school
but they kept asking, so I answered with *flowers, Korean nail polish*.

I am glad for keeping this inconsequential secret because
my grandma and I were walking back to her apartment complex

named Sunshine Village. She pointed to a flower bush tucked
behind green fences and ordered me to grab as many as I could.

When my small hands fumbled, she pushed me aside and did it herself.
Instructing me to keep an eye on the security man's booth

because he gave her a warning the last time. I don't want
to explain the crushed petals, Saran Wrap, her spit on my nails.

This is when I learned I liked to take things not for sale.
There was no wisdom or love when my grandma pressed

the sweet mixture against fingertips. Only *sit still, don't touch
anything*. Hours later, she held my hands to the light, making sure

the sunset stain would last all the way back as she squeezed
my Saran-Wrapped fingertips, stamping me with her dojang.

FALSE TEETH

My father's gums are smooth plateaus.

From sledgehammer bites of his yellowed molars,

he crushed ice into pixie dust.

When I was four, I opened my mouth

for soft crystals across my tongue.

I still pretend to understand how you let

your teeth chip away and my mouth chatters

with windup teeth—pushing them out

with my tongue onto the sink next to yours.

ODE TO WANTING TO RUN OVER OTHER PEOPLE'S CHILDREN IN THE CHURCH PARKING LOT

My sister is confused. Wants a cell phone,
a Chanel bag, an iPad, tickets to the Governors Ball.

The list grows every Sunday. Crying,
perplexed by wants she didn't know she wanted.

I tease her about how she's only eight
but she is betrayed, says I don't get it.

I tell my mom Michelle is going crazy here.
We walk to the van, all smiles and bows

to the church people saying that *us country
folk from Indiana will get used to the city*

soon. I have already downloaded pictures
of the red-bricked house on a hill

for a Sunday like this. I show my mom these pictures
as we wait for Michelle's friends to charm everyone

with respectful goodbyes. I say loud enough
for Michelle to hear that we could just run

them over. I can't stop laughing because I know
they know that'd make it better.

IN THE MIDDLE OF THE HIGHWAY, THERE IS A GARDEN

No cabbages or beds of blossoming azaleas,
just fourteen rows of loosened soil
sprinkled with chicken and cow manure.
Drop the pruners and sweat-stained hat, slip
off your shoes, and push the rusty wheelbarrow
into traffic—hear the brassy clash and
honks that follow. Sink your toes into the dirt,
bowing underneath the rhythm of your prudent steps
as you bend and reach down, breaking
clumps of dried soil—place a pinch on your tongue to taste.
Better yet, cast my ashes across this garden,
and throw them far, never mind getting me in your hair,
close your eyes and toss.

LOOP SPURS

I check my ledger   full of people   I finally
committed to memory   I don't know   which of these I
want to keep pocket these slips of touch   like stumbling out
        from a muddy hike   a hand at my shoulder   after
a car turns the hill   across the lake a hand   because the
rumble   seemed to come from behind us   I know these
touches   are evolutionary reflexes   but still I imagine them
            so I can say I too have experienced   these
flashes of unsayable intimacy   hover of hand at waist   I could
isolate these moments   pipette them into test tubes
whirl them in a centrifuge   create dissolvable pills to take
        every three days   to maintain this dam or   to
drop into a cup of water   hear each bubble   fizzle away
                revel in how it blurs into a hissing cloud
every time   I need a taste

NEW YEAR'S ON ROCKLAND AVENUE

The pastor stops his sermon
to start the countdown. This year,

God can wait ten seconds to finish.
We've already lined up at ten p.m.,

somber for the bread and blood, stifling
our laughs at the sincerity of it all.

I've curled my sister's hair, highlighted
her cheekbones, put on our sparkly heels

post-selfies, even with our brother. Our friends
ask where we're going. When we say church,

no one believes us. We're surrounded
by Korean banners declaring "Peace on Earth,"

a Christmas tree, a Nativity scene. We send snaps
to our friends, each of us captioning

pictures with the best Jesus jokes. We shake
everyone's hands, glad for the booming echoes

of Korean. We forget how to say
Happy New Year, so my sister exclaims

Happy Birthday instead. We don't have
a family tradition, but we do this every year

even through my mother's lamentations
that her children are straying further

from God. But when I'm home, my sister
still asks if I believe in everything

we grew up with, and I say yes, I do.
I believe in grandmothers in crystal pinks dropping daisies

on the top of my hand on New Year's Eve,
after everyone has prayed for a year's worth

of good blessings. I believe in a patch of grass
turning into a volleyball court, where it's filled

with flittering girls, making flower chains
long as a jump rope asking me to try.

When it breaks, they laugh and make another.
Dutifully munching on Costco cookies

in the church cafeteria after midnight,
when our parents tell us that it's our turn,

we find our brother to tell him it's time to get
our blessings. We lumber up the red carpet

steps to the stage, kneel, wait for the pastor
to say our names with conviction and his hands

on our heads, asking God for a litany of things
our parents wrote on a piece of soft paper.

MY MOTHER ON THE LAVA ROCKS OF JEJUDO

We grasped those pink plumes
tethered by bamboo. Our fans

opened wide with a flick,
obscured everything we wanted.

A gaggle of delicate-footed girls
huddled together, transformed

into a trembling lotus, eager butterflies,
and shapes we'd never seen.

All we did was open ourselves
like peonies reaching for light.

Our fluttering hid our parents' faces
in the crowd. Their pure girls onstage,

hanbok skirting the floor,
a twirl, sliver of white sock,

white shoe, a wave of sea-foam
unfurling against a lifeless beach.

ANOTHER DOOR TO THE MOON

Every time I see something cool
and point it out to someone

it sneaks behind a building,
shrinks itself, camera-shy

So I will capture it here—
the perfect crescent of the first

clipped nail stained orange
from peeling tangerines

while we watched TV again,
held each other again, having not

gone outside we wonder
what the moon looks like today

but don't bother peeking out the blinds
because it's always the same

Instead I tell you about a childhood song
about the night sky—how my face is round and big

like the moon but the only Korean word
I can remember is the word for *egg*,

for *daughter*, 달걀 and 딸,
when the word is so simple

I forgot about it entirely and instead
think *door*, which is 문, which yes,

sounds like *moon*, and I finally whisper
to you 달, and there it is, there's the 달.

ACKNOWLEDGMENTS

I am deeply grateful to the editors of the publications where these poems first appeared:

BOAAT: "The Cheonyeo Gwishin Marries Me"

The Cincinnati Review's miCRo series: "사랑니: (n) wisdom teeth"

Colorado Review: "봉숭아: (n) Garden Balsams, Touch-Me-Nots"

Crab Orchard Review: "After the Burial, the Dead Take Everything that Burns"

Electric Literature: "Ode to the New York Heatwave" and "Bowl of Fat"

The Evansville Review: "Urgent Care"

Four Way Review: "Hello, My Parents Don't Speak English Well, How Can I Help You?"

Gulf Coast: "Remember This When You're Hungry"

Hobart: "The Symmetry of Fish," "Diorama," and "Tonight I Discover Archipelagos"

The Journal: "Winters in Queens"

New England Review: "How to Say Water" and "Abecedarian for ESL in West Lafayette, Indiana"

Orion: "My Mother on the Lava Cliffs of Jejudo"

PANK: "Fermented"

Pleiades: "The Old Man in White has Given My Mother a Ripe Persimmon Again"

Poetry: "가시: (n) thorn, splinter, fishbone," "My Bed Shakes and I Assume the Ghosts Are Finally Getting Me," "밤 (v) to give death (n) chestnut, night," and "A Little Cheonyeo Gwishin Appears in My Kitchen"

The Shore: "Aubade with Metal Spoon" and "At an Apple Orchard in Door County, Wisconsin"

Southeast Review: "New Year's on Rockland Avenue"

Southern Indiana Review: "The Sun and Moon Began with a Mother Working"

Sugared Water: "According to My Father, Peaches Ward Off Spirits" and "In the Middle of the Highway, There is a Garden"

Thrush Poetry Journal: "Tangerine Trees & Little Bags of Sugar"

This book would not be in your hands without everyone who has taken the time to read my work, but more important, those who spent time with me during the years this book was in the making. Everything I learned about writing and community building was made possible by love and patience.

First, I would like to thank all of my teachers.

To Molly Brodak, the first person who not just told me but showed me that I could *be* a poet, that being a poet could be a life, that this was possible for me. All I wanted was to gift you my first book, *this* book, because I wouldn't be here without your kindness and patience.

To those who were there early on when I needed so much guidance: Laura Otis, Natasha Trethewey, and Kevin Young during my time at Emory. To those whose conversations and time spent in committees helped this book become what it is: Kimberly Blaeser, Cathy Bowman, Liam Callanan, Brenda Cárdenas, Rebecca Dunham, Ross Gay, Gwynne Kennedy, and Adrian Matejka.

To my friends, Marianne Chan, Anni Liu, Lisa Low, and Danni Quintos—thank you for always pushing me to write, for seeing my early drafts of so many of these poems for what they could become. To Rachel McCabe and Samantha Tett, to Maggie Su and Scott Fenton—for our many memories in Bloomington. To CJ Scruton and Danielle Koepke—for our debriefs over cheese curds and burgers. To Jessie Roy and Whitney Pow—for not only encouraging me but also teaching me how to champion others.

To everyone who's taught me how to be in the literary world—you know who you are. To all the editors I've worked with and who have ushered my poems and this book into the world. A special thank-you to my incredibly generous editor, Allie Merola. You helped me see this book in a new light and the care you took with my work means so much more than I can describe here.

To my family, for showing me everything I know about love and compassion.

To my dearest Kia Xiong, thank you for being there for me through life and for championing my writing and teaching me generosity and joy.

Finally, to Anthony Correale—you always show me what words on a page can build in the real world and, most important, for the love you show to be multifaceted and always surprising.

PENGUIN POETS

GAROUS
ABDOLMALEKIAN
Lean Against This Late Hour

PAIGE ACKERSON-KIELY
Dolefully, A Rampart Stands

JOHN ASHBERY
Selected Poems
Self-Portrait in a Convex
  Mirror

PAUL BEATTY
Joker, Joker, Deuce

ZEINA HASHEM BECK
O

JOSHUA BENNETT
Owed
The Sobbing School
The Study of Human Life

TED BERRIGAN
The Sonnets

LAUREN BERRY
The Lifting Dress

JOE BONOMO
Installations

PHILIP BOOTH
Lifelines:
  Selected Poems
  1950–1999
Selves

JIM CARROLL
Fear of Dreaming:
  The Selected Poems
Living at the Movies
Void of Course

SU CHO
The Symmetry of Fish

RIO CORTEZ
Golden Ax

ALISON HAWTHORNE
DEMING
Genius Loci
Rope
Stairway to Heaven

CARL DENNIS
Another Reason
Callings
Earthborn
New and Selected Poems
  1974–2004
Night School
Practical Gods
Ranking the Wishes
Unknown Friends

DIANE DI PRIMA
Loba

STUART DISCHELL
Backwards Days
Dig Safe

STEPHEN DOBYNS
Velocities:
  New and Selected Poems
  1966–1992

EDWARD DORN
Way More West

HEID E. ERDRICH
Little Big Bully

ROGER FANNING
The Middle Ages

ADAM FOULDS
The Broken Word:
  An Epic Poem of the
  British Empire in Kenya,
  and the Mau Mau Uprising
  Against It

CARRIE FOUNTAIN
Burn Lake
Instant Winner
The Life

AMY GERSTLER
Dearest Creature
Ghost Girl
Index of Women
Medicine
Nerve Storm
Scattered at Sea

EUGENE GLORIA
Drivers at the Short-Time Motel
Hoodlum Birds
My Favorite Warlord
Sightseer in This Killing City

DEBORA GREGER
In Darwin's Room

TERRANCE HAYES
American Sonnets for
  My Past and Future Assassin
Hip Logic
How to Be Drawn
Lighthead
Wind in a Box

NATHAN HOKS
The Narrow Circle

ROBERT HUNTER
Sentinel and Other Poems

MARY KARR
Viper Rum

WILLIAM KECKLER
Sanskrit of the Body

JACK KEROUAC
Book of Blues
Book of Haikus
Book of Sketches

JOANNA KLINK
Circadian
Excerpts from a Secret
  Prophecy
The Nightfields
Raptus

JOANNE KYGER
As Ever: Selected Poems

ANN LAUTERBACH
Hum
If in Time: Selected Poems
  1975–2000
On a Stair
Or to Begin Again
Spell
Under the Sign

PENGUIN POETS